THE EVERYDAY JOURNEY

In loving memory of my parents,
Billy and Clare FitzGerald

Betty Maher

The Everyday Journey

MOMENTS OF REFLECTION

the columba press

First published in 2001 by
the columba press
55A Spruce Avenue, Stillorgan Industrial Park,
Blackrock, Co Dublin

Cover by Bill Bolger
Photograph by Sr Soubirous (Ann) FitzGerald IBVM
Photograph copyright Betty Maher
Origination by The Columba Press
Printed in Ireland by ColourBooks Ltd, Dublin

ISBN 1 85607 346 7

Contents

Introduction

These reflections are in part based on radio programmes which have been broadcast on RTE's 'Living Word' and Lyric FM's 'Quiet Quarter' during the intervening years since my book, *Woman Journeying*, was published in 1994. As with *Woman Journeying*, I have re-written each piece, adapting it for the eye rather than the ear.

In Part One I have looked at the interconnectedness of each human being with every other and at the way in which this co-dependency allows us to impart to one another the very stuff, the breath of life, which keeps us going.

In Part Two I have looked at our co-dependency on every other created thing in the universe, without which we could not be.

At the end of Part One I have added some reflections on ministry, since it is often through such ministry that we most acutely experience our co-dependency. We are always on one side or the other: either in such robust health that we are in a position to minister to others, or at the receiving end – and if not today, then surely tomorrow. Taking this angle, it seems to me that to live a human life is to be involved in ministry.

I am very conscious that many have experienced difficulty, as I have, in finding a place in a named ministry in the official order of things within some churches. Writing about those difficulties has helped to clarify in part some of these matters for me and may perhaps also prove useful to others. But I intend that there be a note of hope also because, despite the barriers which man-made rules have imposed in this area, it is my wholehearted belief that there can be no gainsaying the Holy Spirit, who will blow where She will.

At the end of Part Two I have written something of my own experience of prayer, and I hope that this is not arrogant. For what they are worth, they are my thoughts on what often seems to me to be the difficulty of praying, while at the same time I try to acknowledge that if I could perhaps recognise those gifted moments – those sudden, unexpected glimpses of beauty perhaps, or of love – for what they are, then such recognition in itself, and the heartfelt gratitude which they invoke, may well turn out to be the simplest and possibly the most authentic prayer of all.

Finally, I am convinced that, on a journey, fellowship matters. Many of the fellowships which I have been privileged to enjoy have brought to my life both vitality and colour. To those who have accompanied me, with varying degrees of patience and impatience, my heartfelt thanks. Because of them I continue to dare to hope.

Foreword

To be human is to be connected to others. Nothing can be more true than that 'no man is an island'. Throughout our lives we are dependant on one another.

Again, it is only human that some of these connections will be more important to us than others. Particular people, for each of us, often give our lives meaning and their presence is, as I see it, a sign of what we can hope for in eternity.

But there is also a more general interconnectedness into which we, and all of creation, are inextricably woven, and I cannot get away from this overall interconnectedness. Everything I see, hear, touch, or come in contact with in any way reminds me of, connects me to, something else.

And this includes people I may never have known face to face. I think it works like this: I know a certain number of people and each of those people knows a certain number of others; so, through the person I know, I am connected, even if in a seemingly tenuous way, to the people he or she knows, even though there may be oceans between us and even though we may never meet.

And all of this, I believe, means that in a very real sense every man, woman and child, since he or she is connected to me, really is my brother or sister.

Now, the historians are agreed that Jesus did exist, at a certain time and in a certain place. He, too, was a member of the human race. Therefore he too is connected to each of us, and we to him, just as we are to each other.

If, on top of all of that, I happen to be a Christian – that is, if I believe that Jesus, Son of God, was also fully human – then it must follow that I believe that I am intimately connected to Jesus through our common humanity. When I can grasp and hold on to the belief – even if only fleetingly – that Jesus Christ, Son of God *and* fully human, subject to the same joys and sorrows, delight and pain, hopes and fears to which I am subject, is intimately connected to me, then I can dare to hope.

And I can dare to hope precisely because if this same Jesus, my brother in humanity, is also the Son of God, then I am in an extraordinary position with regard to my Maker; then I, and every other human being that ever existed or that ever will exist, am for ever intimately connected to that same infinite Godhead. And surely from such a point it is not too far a leap to reach the point of believing that there is something indestructable in each of us, and that eventually 'all shall be well, and all manner of thing shall be well'.

And through this same infinity, common to all of us, I am drawn to the conclusion that all our journeys are in some extraordinary way a part of the whole, a part of the great overall adventure in which the indomitable Spirit, the Essence through which we live and move and have our being, moves with and in all of us and, further, it must follow that through this same Spirit we will all eventually be united, in love, with the only Absolute.

This, then, is the belief in which I dare to pin my hope.

PART ONE

Human Fellowship: Stuff of Life

Continuity

Several years ago, before the waiting list became as long as it is today, I was one of a party of four who went to Newgrange for the winter solstice.

Only two of the four actually had tickets to enter the chamber but in those days, before the Interpretative Centre was built, if you hadn't a ticket to get you into the actual chamber you could still enter the field and could therefore enjoy the marvellous atmosphere and the sense of awe which surrounds the place. Hence we were four.

On this particular morning the sun couldn't penetrate the clouds and we had to be satisfied with the simulated light coming through the ope over the entrance, but such was the delight of everyone at being there that no one seemed to mind. And I found it very moving to be caught into the mystery not only of the extraordinary genius of those who had built such a place so long ago, but also to stand on the same ground – bone dry ground, since no rain had ever penetrated it – inside the chamber, where others had stood all of five thousand years ago, and goodness knows on how many occasions in between. And it was clear that I was not the only one sensing this mystery; even after the event no one was in a hurry to leave.

I have been back to Newgrange on numerous occasions since then and in all seasons, and I always love it, but there was one other occasion which has imprinted itself on my mind.

It was on an ordinary autumn day and on a date of no particular significance, and I unexpectedly found myself there in the company of someone who had come, so he said, twelve thousand miles, to visit, amongst other places, the grave of a mutual and much loved friend. He was a stranger to me, except for the fact that we had recently corresponded and made phone calls prior to his arrival, in order to set up a meeting.

It so happened that our mutual friend had been one of the original party of four at the time when I first visited Newgrange; she had in fact been the main instigator of that outing. Now, several years later, the intrepid traveller from Australia and I had gone to Newgrange on the spur of the moment; one instant we had been visiting our friend's grave, and the next we found ourselves heading for Co Meath. What astonished both of us was that in the phonecalls and correspondence during the weeks beforehand the possibility of a visit to Newgrange hadn't once surfaced. Yet this is where we were now heading.

And all of this increased my sense of wonder. True, I was still fascinated by the many mysteries which surround the chamber and its environs, but now there was a further dimension; now I was aware of an extraordinary connectedness. Here we were, myself a 'local', and this man from so far away; and all the while both of us acutely conscious – and fully aware that the other was acutely conscious – of our deceased friend, who had stood with me in Newgrange just a few short years earlier.

To all of this I added the thought of the myriads of people who had, over so many millennia, stood in just this place, and I felt at that moment that we were living through a very tangible example of the interconnectedness of the whole human race, both living and dead. I was imbued with a keen awareness of the meaning of the phrase 'the communion of saints' – that is, saints with a small 's', which many believe connects each of us to the other.

And I believe that such experiences are not completely rare. I believe that they occur, in some shape or form, more often perhaps than we might think. The trick, it seems to me, is to be open to them when they do occur.

Another example comes to my mind: Father Michael Sweetman, a gentle Jesuit who used to contribute regularly to a two-minute reflective radio programme on RTÉ, 'A Living

Word', was a person who always seemed open to such possibilities. Once, he told of a journey he had made several years earlier on an ocean liner crossing the Atlantic. On deck he fell into conversation with two women and, according to him, this chance conversation turned out to be so life-giving to all three that even as he told the story several years later he was able to say with complete conviction, 'The conversation is not over yet.'

And this made sense to me. As with the traveller from Australia, as with our deceased friend, the distances between us did not bring everything to an end. Some conversations, some friendships, because of their very essence, their very stuff, are made to last.

And such stories, too, make me wonder if there can be such things as co-incidences. This next story, which I heard several years ago, still leaves me wide-eyed:

Two friends of mine – we'll call them John and Sheila – went to Australia on holiday. Before they set out, another friend of theirs asked them to look up an old sweetheart of his who had emigrated to Sydney some twenty years earlier and they promised to do so.

On their arrival in Sydney they telephoned the woman's house – we'll call her Mary – only to be told by her daughter that Mary had left Australia on an extended holiday. So, that was that.

On their way back to Ireland my two friends stopped over in Singapore for a couple of nights. There they separated, one to go shopping, another to see the sights.

The sight-seer was soon exhausted, and she made her way into a MacDonald's Restaurant, where she felt the food and the language would be familiar. While she was sitting there she took out a map, to try and orientate herself a little in this strange city. Near her there was a woman of about her own age who looked European, drinking coffee. After a few moments that woman addressed my friend, and asked her if she might glance at the map, since she had left hers at her hotel. Thus they fell into conversation.

My friend – Sheila – introduced herself and said that she was from Ireland. The other woman then said, 'I'm Irish too.' Then Sheila explained further how she came to be in Singapore at that moment but before she had got very far into her story the other woman, Mary, suddenly said, 'Do you mind telling me your name?'

My friend did so, whereupon Mary reached into her pocket and took out a letter. She said, 'I got this from my daughter in Sydney this morning; this is how it begins: "You have just missed John and Sheila from Dublin. They were here on holiday, and had hoped to meet you".'

So, here in the teeming city, on possibly the only occasion in their lives that either of these women would find themselves in this place, Sheila and Mary had come face to face 'by accident', as they sat drinking coffee in a restaurant.

I don't know what that story means, but when I remember it, it cuts right to the core of my sense of wonder and strengthens my belief that there is something other than chance at work.

Such happenings, such conversations and friendships as I have described above, are at least part of the reason why I can, at least at times, believe that we are all moving towards unity. I feel that through these extraordinary – or very ordinary – happenings we are given glimpses of that communion for which we all long, and towards which we aspire.

Forgotten Dreams

I trudged up the hill, and not for the first time. But this time I was more hopeful; this time, knowing the pitfalls from previous attempts, I had come armed with an old map and therefore felt on surer ground.

At least, surer with regard to success in my quest to pick out the old house from the others which stood near it. But I still had reasons to be apprehensive. For example, would the present incumbents welcome me? Would they even understand why I had felt so drawn to the place? Could I expect anyone else to understand why I wished to walk on the same ground, step inside the same stone walls as my forebears had done a century before?

And then I got my first pleasant surprise. The present owner spotted me and her greeting was friendly. Encouraged, I explained what had brought me there, and her friendliness turned to genuine warmth. She bade me enter, and together we toured the house, upstairs and down. We drank tea together and discussed the fact that the house had once had an Anglo-Saxon name superimposed on the original Irish one, and that it had been my grandparents who had changed it back again.

And then I received my second lovely surprise. 'Feel free to wander wherever you like, on you own,' she said. 'Take another look upstairs, and be sure to walk through the garden, it's lovely – and especially at this time of the year.'

I did all of those things. And in the garden I sat on a very old stone wall looking into the distance and imagining my grandmother – whom I had barely known, and never in this place – sitting just here, at the turn of the last century. I imagined her as a young woman, pushing her bicycle up the steep hill and the exhilaration she must have felt the first time she free-wheeled down that hill into the streets of the city below. In those restrictive times for women, how marvellous it must have been to find such freedom, even for a little while.

And I was conscious of just how little – despite appearances – our lives change, from generation to generation. We still have the same responsibilities, the same work to do; still carry the same worries; still experience the same joys and sorrows. The human condition is both timeless and universal.

Sunk in reverie, the young boy of the house had come up beside me before I realised he was there. About 14 or 15 years old, at a guess, he was tall and thin and looked as if he had just sprouted a foot or two in the previous few months. He had an open, smiling face. He held out his hand. 'I'm Michael', he said simply. And then he continued, 'I thought you might like me to show you the garden. It's beautiful.'

I thanked him and we wandered along the mossy path, ducking under some low-slung branches of fruit trees. I was amazed at his knowledge.

'This is a Cox's Pippin', he said, and all the while he spoke quite unaffectedly. 'And this is a Granny Smith. All of these trees are over a hundred years old.' And then he added smiling, 'Your grandparents must have planted them.'

He continued conducting the tour. 'We've black and red currants over here, and gooseberry bushes there. And over here I'm growing cabbages, onions and lettuce.'

We stopped then by another low wall and sat down and looked at the wide river and the city far below us. Michael pointed out the various spires and towers to me, remarking on which of the landmarks would have been there in my grandparents' time and which would have been built in the interim. I was astounded by his knowledge, but even more by the simple and unaffected manner with which he imparted that knowledge to me.

As our tour came to an end I said, 'I gather you like living here, Michael.' He stopped in his tracks and gave me a great smile. 'Like it!' he said, 'I absolutely love it!' And then he added,

'The truth is, I can't imagine ever living anywhere else in the whole world.'

I came away from that visit with an enormous feeling of peace, because I knew that at least for the present the lovely old house was in the safest of hands.

Love's Labour

Sometimes I visit a house beside a lake, right at the water's edge, a house which more than thirty years ago I had seen in the making. I had been present at the laying of the foundations and knew the love that had gone into each row of bricks lovingly put in place by those who revelled in the peace and tranquility of that particular corner of the midlands. I had watched them as they watched their dream come true.

One of the greatest joys for me in revisiting this house is the sight, as I round the bend in the road and it comes newly into view, of the two delicate chestnut trees and the solitary beech tree, all of which stand near the house, giving it shelter. Still young, the trees stand gracefully, as the planter intended, welcoming all who arrive. Each time I see them I bless the planter, now long gone, for his act of faith.

On one particular day a few years ago two of us travelled down to the house for a weekend and within a few moments of arriving walked in the direction of the water's edge. It happened that there was quite a strong breeze blowing and the wind whistled through a copse of small trees which we passed on our way. And as we did so we became aware that there were small blue/grey objects falling to the ground at our feet. We picked some of them up and found them to be tiny, ripe plums.

We were both astonished, my companion even more than I. She was much more intimately connected to the place than I was, but this was the very first time, she said, that she had seen any fruit fall from those trees. We looked carefully at the little copse, and in amongst various other species of trees we counted five plum trees, growing wild, some thirty feet or more high. In fact they were so high that we could only harvest their fruit by shaking the branches and letting the plums fall.

For both of us that was an extraordinary moment. We realised that, unknown even to many of those nearest the project, fruit trees had been planted for the benefit of all who would come after; we were quite literally gathering the fruits of the labours of others.

Generation gap?

The small boy came into the room quietly, carrying a large box of bricks. He scrambled up on to a chair at the table and spilled the bricks on to the cloth which had been put there specially, to cut down on the noise. And then he turned and looked at his grandmother thoughtfully for a moment and said, 'Would you like to play?' 'I would', she replied, getting up from her armchair and moving to the table, and the two of them got to work.

Very little was said between them. Occasionally she would ask if she was following his plan, which was, after all, only in his head. And he would glance up from his own work and look at hers and nod his head. And then another five minutes of silence would pass. Now and then he would reach over and explain to her that she was going a bit off course, and she would adjust the bricks to his satisfaction.

Several minutes went by and then he suddenly stopped building and, looking at her intently he asked her, 'Gran, were you ever a little girl?' 'I was', she said. Another pause, while he studied her face. And then, 'I was thinking that. You play well.' And they both went on with the business in hand.

What makes this story so marvellous to me is that almost thirty years later, as she was reaching the end of a full and busy life, this was the story which she would most often tell, and it was also the story which seemed to give her not only great joy, but also great hope.

And I found it a salutary lesson also, because it seemed to say that we can never know, when we speak to another, just how long our words may stay with that other. And that makes me think that I can never be careful enough when I speak.

Waiting

Perhaps when it comes to waiting, grandparents are tops. They seem to know not only what it is to wait, but there's a good chance also that they have a great understanding of its value. The bustling time of their own lives may be coming to its natural end and now they have a chance to look for a bit longer at the flowers, or at the growing generation; at the clouds scudding across the sky; at the leaves blowing in the wind. And if they are also blessed with a belief, they will know that by taking time out 'just to think', they are indeed in good company. Mary 'pondered in her heart'. Jesus 'went apart'. Joseph gave himself time to think things out, so we are told.

Very often it seems that the first person a pregnant woman will turn to when she realises her condition is another woman who has already been through the same experience. Sometimes it may be her mother. I often think that this may well have been what Mary did. Kahlil Gibran, in his book *Jesus, Son of Man,* falls to pondering the relationship between St Anne and her grandchild. He even suggests that perhaps that same grandchild may not have been the easiest to understand. St Anne was a human grandmother, Jesus a fully human child. It may have been a great relationship, or it could have been a difficult one, either is possible.

Be that as it may, I imagine that Mary may well have relied on her mother for much guidance while awaiting the birth of Jesus. And I'm sure also that when Mary and Joseph had to set out on their long journey just when Mary was coming up to her confinement, her mother must have been worried for them. It may also have put a great physical distance between them.

So, St Anne, too, had to wait. And whether she did this with patience or impatience we cannot know. Perhaps, as may be the case with many expectant grandparents, there may have been anxiety for St Anne during that first Advent. But maybe also her faith was such that she remained undisturbed while awaiting the arrival of her grandchild.

But perhaps also, having her life's experience behind her, she may have had the equanimity to say to her daughter, as Teresa of Avila has said to all of us later on:

Let nothing disturb you,

Let nothing frighten you.

All things pass,

God never changes.

Patience obtains all things.

The one who has God lacks nothing.

God alone suffices.

I think it's a good trick to remember that prayer often, and especially when the going gets rough.

Danny

When I turned the corner of the hospital corridor I saw Danny leaning against the wall, his thin shoulders hunched, their shape protruding through the fabric of his dressing-gown and, although I had only know him as the silent man of the ward, I got the impression this morning that he was waiting for me. And I was right.

'Johnnie' s gone', he said, and his voice was full of woe. Then he continued: '9 o'clock this morning. Just gave a cough and fell back on the pillows. I called a nurse, but he was gone all right. They pulled the curtains then.' He took out a crumpled handkerchief and blew his nose hard.

'I'm very sorry', I said, and could think of nothing else to say.

Silent Danny may have been to most of us, but there had obviously been a bond between himself and Johnnie that a passer-by might have missed.

He spoke again.

'I can't understand it. He seemed well enough earlier on – better than myself. Though, mind you, come to think of it, he did give me half of his bread at breakfast this morning'

And with that Danny turned away from me and shuffled off, the rope of his dressing-gown trailing along the floor behind him. He was a forlorn sight.

Later, I told the story to a friend. He listened in silence and then said quietly, 'And they recognised him in the breaking of the bread.'

And that was a revelatory moment for me, because until he said it I hadn't made the connection.

Patience – with self

I watched the old woman as she negotiated the three shallow steps which separated the two levels of the old street. Her body was knotted and gnarled and she was bent almost double; her arms were twisted into her sides, and she had to grasp the hand rail on the wall with the hand which should have been furthest away from it, but because her mis-shape was nearest. She glanced up at me and I said, with great timidity, because I was afraid of distracting her, 'Are you better managing on your own, or can I help in any way?'

'I'm better on my own' she said, and slowly and painfully she made her way through the same motions on each step, until she reached ground level.

I waited, because it seemed the only thing to do, and then I asked, 'Are the steps the hardest thing?'

She nodded. 'They are', she said, and then with a marvellous smile she added, 'But, sure, I'll just have to put up with myself.' And she actually laughed, before hobbling off.

As I left the spot I was acutely aware of two things: one was the ease with which I could put one foot in front of the other, knowing that my legs would carry me to my destination without my even having to think about it; and the other was more subtle: I realised that her words, 'I'll just have to put up with myself' were in fact saying exactly what Gerard Manley Hopkins said when he wrote, 'My own heart let me more have pity on.'

And it struck me that on days which may be shaping up badly, it might be something to remember.

Otherness

It was a week short of midsummer's day, and Killiney Bay was like a mill pond. The tide was at its most distant point and there wasn't even a sea breeze. Although it was late evening, a few children still played at the water's edge and their parents packed up the picnic things in leisurely fashion. I don't know when I had last seen such clarity in the air. Bray Head and Killiney Hill stood proud to the south, Sugar Loaf behind them, and Sorrento Terrace and Dalkey Island to the north seemed almost near enough to touch. A perfect day.

And, looking down, the stones; the vast array of shapes, sizes, colours and textures. To start to notice them was to be constantly urged into picking one up, and then another, and another. It was simply impossible to gather all that caught the eye and choices had to be made, certain ones discarded in favour of others – impossible decisions!

I was with a friend and our conversation ranged over serious matters, funny matters, heart-warming matters, sorrowful matters. Each of us did our best to understand the other and sometimes we succeeded with ease. At other times, however, clarification was necessary and, above all, intense listening and patience. And at one point I found myself comparing the infinity of the variety of the stones with the very essence of our conversation. There was an infinity in our exchange, and in the mystery of the other, which was always present.

And, with such evidence of infinity, I wondered why it is that we sometimes doubt. Perhaps the answer has to do with being human. And if this is so, then no doubt our very doubting is acceptable, as part of our own truth.

'I'll say, he'll say …'

I was confiding to my great friend my strategy for my next –
needless to say absolutely vitally important – meeting with the
'Significant Other ' in my life at that time.

I told her: 'Well, I'll say …' and I gave her an example. And
then I said, 'And he'll say …' And I gave another example. And I
repeated this three or four times when she suddenly burst out
laughing and exclaimed, 'I hope it keeps fine for you!' I looked at
her perplexed, and then I subsided. Of course, she had seen the
absurdity of the whole situation in a nutshell! How could I possibly know what the other party in the hoped-for conversation
would say, and therefore how could I possibly continue with this
make-believe conversation?

I'm older now. Now, I know of only two certainties: one, that
life is completely uncertain from one moment to the next, and
two, that much as I might like it to be different, there are
umpteen things in this world about which I can do nothing.

I'd like to be able to remember these two points more often,
because when I forget them I champ at the bit, causing myself un-
necessary wear and tear. However, if and when I remember
them I think it does two things: firstly, it frees me from useless
worry, and secondly, and perhaps more importantly, it makes it
possible for me to be open to the fact that the very uncertainty of
life also brings with it the possibility of some marvellous surprises,
and that's no bad thing at all.

Incidently, my wise friend was right: the 'Significant Other'
scotched my argument even before I had got it off the ground.

And I don't know what's to be learned from the fact that, several decades down the road, I recognise, and salute, her wisdom.

Losing the way

We were in the heart, the very centre of the county of Galway and, foolish as it may appear, we were, in fact, entirely lost. We wanted to get to Galway city but somehow or other our meanderings far from the beaten track had caused us to lose our bearings. The road was narrow and winding, with high hedges on either side and there wasn't a signpost in sight.

We met a little girl at the side of the road and asked directions. She stared thoughtfully at us for a few moments and then said 'Where did you come from?' We told her. 'Then go back', she said firmly, 'and start again.'

It turned out to be good advice and I've often thought of it since. There are occasions when we may well find ourselves going down a cul-de-sac and sometimes we can neither believe nor admit to this and so we continue on, only to our own detriment.

I remember telling a friend of mine once that I find I can still walk into certain situations which are exact replicas of situations I have been in before and which have done me no good. Sometimes I seem prepared to continue down a road which – although I am usually not prepared to admit it even to myself – is probably going to land me in trouble.

My friend, however, gave me comfort. When I told her of my foolhardiness she just smiled and said 'That's to show you that you're human!' And then she went on: 'Life's a bit like snakes and ladders; there may be times when we just have to go back to the beginning and start all over again. But if so, what's wrong with that? No harm done. You see, the older you get the easier you'll understand that it's the trying that counts.'

Peaceful places

Perhaps there is nothing quite like the oasis of a city park. One moment you are crossing a busy street in a swirl of deafening traffic and the next, when you step into the park, the sounds will suddenly disappear as if by magic.

Dublin is blessed in its parks. St Stephen's Green is probably the best known, and perhaps the best loved also. On a sunny day it is a riot of colour, not only because of the formal flower-beds but also because of its people, and especially the young in their brightly coloured clothes. On such a day a walk through St Stephen's Green is enough to lift the darkest of moods, I find.

I often think that St Stephen's Green is a continuation of the life and vigour of Grafton Street. Recently I crossed over to the Green just at the top of Grafton Street and I was amazed, as I walked through the entrance arch, at just how light-hearted I felt – and how much a part of the whole picture. Having been born in this city and never having left it for any length of time, this place seemed second nature to me and at that moment I seemed to understand what it is to be rooted in a place. And I was delighted.

Merrion Square is newer to me, because for a long time the public didn't have access to it. Now, however, it is as open as St Stephen's Green, and sometimes when I walk in it I am tempted to think that it may be even more beautiful than the Green. It is far less used, for one thing. And the flower beds seem to be far less formal also. The verdure appears to be thicker and it is certainly true that, once in its centre, all sounds of traffic disappear. It amazes me to realise that just a few yards away from where I am standing, cars and buses thunder by.

I remember sitting on a bench in the middle of Merrion

Square several years ago with a friend of mine who was about to leave the country. I remember looking at the top storeys of the elegant Georgian houses and thinking that they were set far back from the park in order to give the people in the park lots of space. And I remember the heat of the sun, and the fact that we did very little talking as we sat there. There was lots of birdsong and even though we were both sad at the fact that we would soon be far away from each other, the peace of that place at that moment somehow made the parting easier, because somehow or other we both became aware of a third element at play here; there was a sense that such peace and beauty was a part of something far bigger than ourselves – something infinite. And because we could sense infinity at that moment this led us to believe that this parting and, indeed, all separation, can only be temporary.

I fervently hope that this turns out to be right!

'The people who tell us about each other'

'They tell me ...' my friend began. 'Who tell you?' I interrupted. 'They do', he said firmly, 'The people who tell us about each other'.

That phrase has stayed with me over many years and this is because I cannot help but wonder about another's ability to tell someone about me with any accuracy. Certainly a third person can tell another of the factual things – that I broke a leg, or won the lottery, or went on holiday. And no doubt this serves some purpose in keeping someone else somewhat appraised of my life.

It doesn't, however, I would venture to say, impart much knowledge about me myself, me at my very core. And just as well; few of us, I imagine, would particularly want to have our innermost thoughts revealed to others in general conversation. They are often far too private – and, indeed, may also be too painful, for general sharing.

In fact, a lot of the time it may be very difficult to express some of our more painful feelings out loud at all, ever. And that's why I believe that it's one of the greatest blessings anyone could have if there is a person with whom they can sit down and have that person listen, and especially if we are in pain. An encounter with such a person, it seems to me, transcends the everyday; it gives us a glimpse of that part of humanity which is more than finite. And I believe that we can count ourselves lucky if we meet even a few such people in the course of one lifetime.

And that's why I believe such friends should be cherished – precisely because they are so rare.

This can be problematic at times, perhaps for geographical or other reasons, and I have only found one way to deal with the matter of separation from someone I love. I confess that it's not always satisfactory, but it's the best I can do. I try to entrust their wellbeing to that Other, who has given them to me as friends in the first place.

And in so doing I hope that this entrusting is in itself a form of prayer.

Seeking the truth

I turned on the radio, just in time to hear a well-known theologian say, 'I am convinced that when two people are engaged in loving argument, God is there, because the fact that they are so engaged means that there is a deep searching on both their parts for the Truth.'

I could have cheered! For far too long I had been afraid to say to someone I love, 'I don't agree with you'. But in the interest of truth it may sometimes be vital that we 'agree to differ'. Honouring difference, is the way some people describe it.

Such honest discourse, which may at times include profound disagreement, may seem risky, but nonetheless I believe that it is something we must learn. I think it's also fair to say that if we take such a risk, one or other or even both participants may find that they can be 'surprised by joy', because in such honest exchange there is always the possibility of sudden, perhaps marvellous revelation.

And again I cannot help but think of Jesus and the Samaritan woman. Here was a totally honest conversation, she giving as good as she got, in truth and simplicity. 'How come that you, a Jew, speak to me, a Samaritan?' And their exchange: 'Go and tell your husband.' 'I have no husband.' 'You're right there.' Total lack of pretence and no punches pulled on either side.

And we know the result of this unaffected honesty: in the first place, Jesus revealed to her who he was, and secondly, he called her, against all the odds, to direct ministry.

What better example could we have of the value of openness and honesty in our personal relationships?

Fear

The opposite to believing in the interconnectedness of everyone and everything is fear of the Other. Pierre Teilhard de Chardin, Jesuit, writer, theologian, philosopher and much more besides, has this to say about our reaction to things and/or people unknown to us: 'The Other usually appears to be the worst danger that our personality meets in the whole course of its development. The Other must be got out of the way.'

He is, I believe, saying that we are afraid of that which we do not know. And perhaps this is at least part of the reason why there are wars. As we helplessly watch the terrible mass destruction of whole races by other races around the globe today it is worth considering, I think, that much of this may be the result of fear of the Other.

And there seems little enough I can do, apart from giving what paltry material support I may be able to give to help the victims. And I can pray, that's for sure. But in the face of such devastation as we see it and hear about it today, my praying seems feeble enough.

However, I also believe there is one other practical thing I can do: I can examine my own attitude to strangers – people of another race, perhaps, whom I may fleetingly encounter as I walk down a street.

And I can then acknowledge the fear that I may well feel when I meet such strangers. It is probably fair to say that many people have just such a reaction.

The wise ones say that if I can bring myself to acknowledge and accept the truth that I am afraid, then this very acknowledgement will in itself help me to confront my fear. It is only when I reach this point of acknowledgement that I can hope to learn not to fear – or hate – that which I do not know.

It may seem like a very small start, but it is at least that, and for that reason is, I believe, worth trying.

Night Sky

It was a wonderfully clear, balmy night in June and I was in a remote part of the French countryside. It was getting dark – almost as dark as it would get, given the time of year. And, because I was far away from street lights, I knew I would be lucky.

I settled myself down on the flat sunchair, surrounded by the dark and the stillness. I scanned the sky slowly and carefully. The longer I scanned it, the more stars I saw. It's wonderful how, as your eyes grow accustomed to the dark, more and more stars appear.

But I was watching for something else, something specific. I knew from past experience that I would only have to wait at the most about twenty minutes or so before I would see a satellite pass overhead. And if I were really lucky – and patient enough – another would probably appear also, travelling on a different orbit.

And of course it came. It always gives me a shock, even though I've been watching them for years now. Out of nowhere they seem to appear, and this one was calmly traversing the large expanse of sky, left to right. My eyes followed its steady course and I only lost sight of it when I couldn't see far enough to keep it in view.

You know very quickly that you are looking at a satellite and not at a shooting star or even a far-away plane, because of the steady, unblinking way in which it moves across the sky in a wide and steady arc.

A myriad things fascinate me about this moving, man-made object. For one thing, it shines, yet I know that there's no light inside it – it shines simply because it's reflecting the sun which at this moment is on the other side of the globe. And that in itself is nearly mystery enough for me.

But then to that I add the fact that somewhere on that other side it's daytime, and over there people are feeling the heat of the sun, while I am in darkness. The same satellite will pass over them also, but they won't be able to see it, because of the sun. All of this – the satellite, the thought of those others at the other side of the globe, connects me to them not in any haphazard fashion but in a very real way. We are connected, each to the other, no matter how far away we may physically be from one another.

And I can never get away from this thought.

Paying attention

If proof were needed today that we need other people, just walk along any street and count the number of people using mobile phones. While I can understand how useful one would be in certain circumstances, sometimes I am mystified by just how much they are used.

Recently I was in a restaurant with a lively group. We hadn't met for a while, so there was much banter. At the table next to ours it was the same, but two tables away things were very different. The young woman facing me was looking down in silence at her hands, and fiddling with her napkin. I looked at her three companions and to my amazement I saw that each of them was earnestly talking into his own mobile phone. And each conversation was separate; between the four at the table at that moment there was no communication at all.

I found it one of the most depressing scenes I've witnessed in a long time. Were they still at work? But it was late in the evening. Were they phoning home because someone near to each of them was at death's door? If so, they probably wouldn't have been out on the town at all. But why on earth had each of them joined three others for a meal only to ignore one another?

Incongruously perhaps, I began to think of the table fellowship which Jesus loved and practised. And I wondered what he would have made of mobile phones. What difference would it have made, for example, that evening in Emmaus, if any one of the three present had had one? Might the precious moment of the Breaking of the Bread have gone unnoticed?

Reflections on the Ministry of Hospitality

Perhaps the most pertinent of all ministries for those of us caught up in the ordinary everyday things of life is the ministry of hospitality. It is so obvious that it is quite easy to overlook it, and yet sometimes I think that perhaps it is the ministry which is most akin to the ministry of Jesus.

I spent many years actively seeking a place in an 'official' ministry in my own church, to no avail. (I was lay and I was married, wasn't that enough for me?) I would have been glad to have served my church in such a capacity, but it was not to be, for reasons best known to the authority church.

However, the ministry of hospitality is open to all. In fact, I wonder if it is possible to live a full Christian life without being actively involved in this particular ministry, and the opportunities to take part in it fall into our laps, probably on a daily basis.

Take one simple example: take a child going to a parent and asking a question. To stop whatever one is doing in order to give that child your full attention is hospitality in itself. Or perhaps a stranger meets you on the street seeking directions. Taking the time to give those directions is to offer hospitality. A spouse who, after 40 years or more, still carries a cup of tea to the other is caught into the ministry of hospitality. Or a nurse or doctor who stays that one minute longer at a bedside to give a moment's comfort or reassurance; or a friend who will listen to another indefinitely at the end of a phone line; the opportunities are myriad and are not confined only to those who minister in an official capacity in our churches.

One of the best visual expressions of the ministry of hospitality available to us in religious form seems to me to be the image, most commonly interpreted as being a depiction of the Holy Trinity, in the very well known icon painted by Rublev in the fifteenth century. I am aware that in the first instance I may have been attracted to this particular icon because it is that rare thing, an icon which does not have the colour red in it. I often find red a hard colour to live with, and it may well be that the softness of the different shades of browns and blues and greens attracted me to this particular icon in the first place, but the essence of the icon also attracts me greatly.

In it there are three figures sitting round a table and they are offering hospitality – to you and me. The figures are arranged in such a way that there is a space for another – you, me, each and every one of us – to sit at table with them. When contemplating this icon you are drawn into that fourth place by the demeanour of the three figures seated there. Everything about them is open and compassionate, and that they are offering hospitality cannot be doubted.

An extraordinary painting by any standards, and yet could anything be more ordinary, more domestic? A table, figures seated at that table, and food and drink on the table, waiting to be shared. Many of us are daily in the same domestic setting.

When I was young I stayed on occasion with a family in Belgium. That particular friendship has stood the test of time, although the chances to meet are few and far between. A couple of years ago I had such a chance. It is now a family of very large numbers indeed – there are those of my own generation, their children and their children's children, and there are still some uncles and aunts around the place. There are always a few strays too, bringing the numbers up even higher.

When I visited them this time round it was plain to see that the mother was the centre of all the activity. Her day was hectic: meals to be prepared, children to talk to and to listen to and advise, grandchildren to placate, people to be driven here and there. The traffic in and out of the house had to be seen to be believed, and it struck me that one would have needed a traffic warden in the hallway just to keep tabs on the comings and goings.

I am fairly used to large numbers, but this surpassed anything I had seen at home.

What struck me most forcibly was that whenever I entered a room where she was, my hostess left whatever she was doing in order to make herself available to me. I was the comparative stranger or at least the guest, and therefore nothing, it seemed, was more important than that she would give me her full attention. I marvelled at her ability to put into practice, in a household which teemed with life and where there were so many calls on her, this simple but profound act of hospitality. I learned a lot from those few days, watching her openness, not just to all who needed her help but even more by her hospitality to me.

And it seems to me that we can practice this ministry every day, at home and at work, simply by the way in which we receive those whom we encounter in the course of an ordinary day. If we live with another, at any level, then it is almost inevitable that we will be called upon to practice it.

And perhaps those of us with families are particularly lucky in this regard. A friend of mine said to me many years ago, 'If you're once from a big family, you're always from a big family.' I think she had a point. There is a constant coming and going, no matter even if one's immediate offspring have flown the nest. To be ready to do whatever is next required is to put the ministry of hospitality into practice. Sometimes it may call upon all our resources to be open and spontaneous in this way, but at least the chances present themselves. How we respond to those chances is what counts.

The gospel stories are full of examples of hospitality. Take the story of Jesus' encounter with the woman at the well. As I understand it, he asks her for a drink, effectively calling on her to minister to him. She responds, and in return for a drink he offers her 'living water' – all she will need to start life afresh. And, indeed, not only that, but he also calls her to direct public ministry at that moment: 'Go and tell the others.' What could be clearer?

There is another wonderful aspect to this particular ministry, in that it is almost invariably reciprocal. You give, and in return you receive onehundredfold. One of the most beautiful stories of hospitality I have ever heard I heard on radio several years ago. A priest told of a young boy – we'll call him John – who, because he found conventional learning somewhat difficult, didn't reach the age at which he was deemed ready to receive his First Communion until he was in his late teens. When the day finally dawned there was great joy among his family and friends when the celebrant – the teller of the story – invited John to approach the altar accompanied by his mother. The two of them walked to the altar rails and the celebrant lifted up a host from the ciborium. 'Receive the Body of Christ, John', he said, handing the host to John. John took it into his hands and bowed. And then, without any warning to anybody, he turned to his mother standing beside him, broke the host in two, and handed half to her, as he said, 'Mammy, receive the Body of Christ.' The celebrant/storyteller told his audience that never before had he been so aware of the mystery and meaning of Eucharist.

I remember too, reading of a woman who had planned to spend Easter week in a monastery, in order to fully participate in the Easter ceremonies. But just as the week began she had a phonecall from a friend asking if she might come to stay, and bring her rather sickly child with her. So much for the Easter ceremonies, the woman thought.

As it happened, on Holy Thursday the child became feverish. Instead of attending the ceremony of the washing of the feet, the woman found herself sitting by the bedside of the sick child, bathing her hot forehead, and as she did so she suddenly realised that here, at this simple, practical level, she was in fact more bound up on the Holy Thursday message than she ever could have been had she gone to the church service that evening. And she realised at the same time that her hospitality to her friend and the sick child had been repaid a hundredfold.

In any story of hospitality I am struck by this element of reciprocity. It occurs again and again. Recently I read and studied the beautiful catalogue attaching to a project of Chris Doris, artist-in-residence of Mayo County Council, who in the summer of 1999 embarked on a unique pilgrimage, spending 40 days and 40 nights at the summit of Croagh Patrick. So beautiful were his written pieces in the catalogue, telling of his encounters with all those who climbed the Reek during those 40 days and nights, that I felt compelled to make the journey to Westport to see the paintings for myself, and it was a feast for the eyes. For the most part they consist of large, perpendicular lines of colour, sometimes of very delicate shades, at other times much stronger, and are, according to the brochure, '... the basic structure of the Croagh Patrick pilgrimage, the endless pattern of ascent and descent'. The changes of colour reflect the changes in the light and colour which he experienced while on the mountain. And he explains that while the work of an artist necessitates spending much time alone, such was the hospitality of those other pilgrims (approximately six thousand during the time he was there) as they came bearing gifts of food, or water, or anything else they felt he might be glad of, he was fully drawn into responding to that generosity. He describes it thus: 'This proximity of a private and quite personal journey to a largely unbounded public exposure renovated the boundaries I habitually hold, and was liberating'. And he continues, 'Their [the other pilgrims'] diversity, openness and support were invigorating.'

As it happened, I had the opportunity to speak to Chris Doris about the reciprocity which I felt flowed between him and those who climbed the Reek during his time there, and his first response was that while he felt that he did indeed receive much hospitality, he wondered as to whether or not he had actually reciprocated this. I said that this was what had come over to me, when reading his written pieces and after some discussion he acknowledged that this might perhaps be so; that perhaps he had returned their hospitality by the very fact of his presence on the mountaintop to greet people when they arrived.

I felt, too, that the actual paintings indicated this: continuous movement up and down, depicting the constant line of pilgrims making their way to and from the summit. There is a fluidity in each painting – all of which are untitled, to allow for different interpretations – save for the overall title of The Pilgrim Series. Having climbed the Reek on several occasions in the past, the paintings and the whole Art Project brought the idea of pilgrim and pilgrimage into a newer, clearer perspective for me, and in particular this lovely example of hospitality demonstrated yet again to me how it is always possible to be surprised by joy, at unexpected times and in unexpected places, if only we are open to such possibilities.

And, as always happens when I begin to think about hospitality, I find myself thinking about friendship, because it is in friendship, I believe, that hospitality is at its best. In friendship there is always the possibility of being surprised, even delighted, by the other. We can never completely know someone else, and that's why such surprise is possible. Someone else's thoughts or actions can veer off in a direction which I myself might never be able to envisage, even in my wildest dreams. And this difference is, to me, the very stuff of life, and that which makes life so enriching. I remember reading somewhere, many years ago, that love and friendship between two human beings best mirrors the love of God for us, and I believe this.

Of course it also follows, must follow, that the difference between two persons means too that there will probably be times when everything may not run smoothly. But what of that? It can often be, I believe, that in the very cut and thrust of trying to sort out differences, delight lies. It follows, too, that such cut and thrust has to be part and parcel of the search of each one for the Truth, so a friend with whom one can debate and tease out arguments is surely a friend indeed. Again, I am reminded of what I once heard Timothy Radcliffe OP, the Head of the Dominican Order, say: 'Where two people are locked in loving argument, there God is to be found, because there is a searching for the truth'.

Of course, such argument does not always make for a peaceful life. There may be times of profound disagreement, sometimes even causing bewilderment and hurt. Real friendship, real love, has to make room for real difference.

And we have a perfect example of this when we look at the relationships which Jesus had with others. Peter, that Rock, was certainly very different in temperament from Jesus, from what we know. Yet Jesus was able to recognise in Peter a level of trustworthiness so strong that he could be left in charge. What greater proof of friendship or love can there be?

And then I am again reminded of the woman at the well, she who was not afraid to speak her mind, even though everything she had learned in life would have warned her against speaking to this stranger. Yet such was the trust Jesus had in her that he involved her too, against all the odds, in spreading his word.

I often wonder about how some friendships will remain active for a whole life-time, but others may fade away over time. Life, with all its vagaries, often leads people in different directions, as a result of which parting becomes inevitable; this parting, I believe, is often more fallen into than deliberately sought out, and it seems to be part of being human.

Inevitably, too, when speaking of friendship, one has to think also of betrayal. This is much harder to withstand than a mere drifting away. Again taking Peter as an example, Jesus, being the type of person he was, forgave Peter not just once but several times. For most of us that may be easier said than done. If we confide our greatest secrets, the longings of our hearts maybe, to another and then find ourselves betrayed, this is a difficult thing to come to terms with. And yet humanity is very frail and I do not believe that anyone can be completely sure that at no time, no matter what the circumstances, will we ever fail a friend. Because we are human, such possibility is always there.

And so, I suppose, allowing for this human frailty is the greatest trust, the greatest act of friendship of all. I love someone, I entrust him or her with the secrets of my life, and yet I know that that person, like me, is human, with all the frailty that that implies. Yet, still, I trust. And there is something in that hope and trust that for me makes the greatest case for life beyond this earthly one. At some extraordinarily deep level we long for complete reliability, we long for utter union of hearts and minds, with no possibility of betrayal. And our most important friend-ships, I believe, manifest for us this perfect state towards which we are always drawn. Our friends are mirrors of what is to come, leading us, like signposts, to the oneness of all creation with the Creator.

When I was in my late teens I had a friend of my own age whose first language was not English, and for that very reason much effort, on both our parts, went into sustaining that friend-ship. We took great care in translating our words as we often dis-cussed with great intensity matters which we saw then – and might, indeed, had things been different, well see now – so that we could fully understand the other's point of view. It was worth the effort, and the friendship held firm over the next twenty years or so until he, his wife and two of his four offspring were wiped out in a senseless car crash. We had managed to meet only very occasionally after we both married in our respective coun-tries, but we managed to in keep in touch by letter and would still argue a point, even on paper, if need be.

When he died I was at a loss; I felt that that particular convers-ation had come to a woeful end. But I was wrong, and I have since discovered that the conversation has not ended even yet. The fact is that sometimes, for no apparent reason, I will remem-ber something he said about a particular subject and I find that even now, all these decades later, his comment will have some influence on me and on my thought process. Perhaps that is the real beauty of friendship: it is never fully over.

Thus do we minister to one another in love and friendship, as I see it, and hospitality is often the visible manifestation of that ministry, which for the most part goes unnamed.

However, there are those whose life's work is in such min-istry and who find it necessary sometimes to withdraw – just as the artist Chris Doris did – but for most of us it will probably take a simpler form. Without going to the lengths to which he went, even if we only take time out now and then to be quiet, to read or to write or to pray, or even just to be, only then may it be possible for us to give our full attention to another.

There are some religious houses who extend simple hospitality to those who want to spend time on their own. It is possible to take a room for a day or more, and to retreat. Sometimes I think that this gesture of hospitality on the part of religious houses may well be one of the best ways for a religious order to help the rest of us in today's noisy world. Because of the frantic activity which manifests itself at every hand's turn today in the market-place, a place of peace and quiet is surely something of enormous value.

It is worth planning to spend a day in such a place, I believe. It is wonderfully refreshing to go apart even for a few hours and leave the daily worries – and chores – behind. It can be quite daunting at first, and may take a little time to settle down and quiet the spirit. But I often think that to make the effort to be in such a place for the specific purpose of withdrawing from the daily hassle will bring with it its own grace; even the doing of it will dispose us to being quieter. And only by being quieter can we listen; it gives us the chance to listen to our hearts and the possibility of discernment.

I am very aware that such time spent alone will be a luxury for many, and that there are those whose daily commitments may be such that this sort of space for themselves is an impossibility. Writing of it here I am thinking more of those of us who might, with a little thought and organisation, manage to try to find space for such a day, simply be re-arranging a few appointments. I believe it is worth making the effort.

And if we do manage to arrange such time for ourselves, then we are in good company: Mary took the time to 'ponder'; Joseph took time to think things out; and Jesus himself, we are told on several occasions, 'went apart'. Such time to ourselves can be the source of renewed life, making it possible for us to enter re-freshed into the everyday ministry to which we are all called at one level or other, that of hospitality.

Pastoral Care: The life-long apprenticeship

Almost a decade and a half ago, just after I had done my hospital chaplaincy training, I was asked to speak to a group of doctors and nurses, in a hospice setting, on the subject of 'Some spiritual aspects of Dying'. I was terrified at the prospect, because I felt that I had seen only the tip of the ice-berg, had only begun to understand the smallest modicom of the subject. And my first instinct was to run from the invitation.

I thought about it for a while, however, and eventually realised that of all ministries, pastoral care is the one where anyone engaged in it will always be an apprentice. I do not believe that anyone, no matter what his or her qualifications, can ever say, 'I am now a fully qualified pastoral carer.' The fact is that in pastoral care, as in life itself, the learning goes on for ever because there are always new things happening. And because of this realisation I undertook the assignment, and for the same reason I dare to write a little about the subject now.

Just as I believe that those who offer hospitality emulate Jesus, so do I believe that those in pastoral care do likewise. And it would seem to me that there is no other way to be in this ministry, because, more than anywhere else, it is here that one is meeting the most vulnerable. Two of the stories which I particularly like, in John's and Luke's gospels respectively, are, firstly, the story of the time that Jesus was asked, 'Where do you live?' and he replied, 'Come and see!' and the second is of the time when he asked his disciples, 'Who do you say that I am?'

It seems to me that in both instances it was by his way of life that Jesus attracted people to him, not by imposing his views on them. In many ways this is a far cry from some of the evangelising practices of the Christian churches in the not-too-distant past. Then, as a recent interview on TV with an elderly missionary amply demonstrated, there was a widespread belief that people who were not Christians should be made to listen [to us] 'whether they like it or not'! Happily, today we have (it is to be hoped) made progress in our understanding of the human psyche and in our continued search for the truth through theology, and it is now generally believed that it is far better to take people 'where they are', to use today's phrase. And it seems to me that this was the more gentle approach taken by Jesus himself, as the two stories above demonstrate.

But nowhere, as I see it, is it more evident that we must try to understand people from their own position than when we find ourselves in the role of a pastoral carer in a hospital. The most obvious reason for this is that when someone is hospitalised that person is a captive audience – an unenviable position at the best of times, worse still when one is ill. A sick person is already at his or her most vulnerable, and in a hospital setting, away from familiar people and familiar surroundings and bombarded perhaps by frightening events, is all the more so.

Consider then what it must be like if at such a time a complete stranger comes to your bedside uninvited. Yet such, often, is the role of the pastoral carer.

Seen in this light, it is hardly surprising that the well known writer Henri Nouwen likens that particular role to that of a clown in a circus: never quite sure where exactly he/she should be, and always on the fringe. It is an apt description. And yet despite this I cannot think of a more privileged position in which to be, nor can I think of any situation when sensitivity is more badly needed.

During my chaplaincy training I often found it necessary to break one rule, and that concerned the amount of time spent at the side of a patient's bed. I could not see how such time could be measurable, and there were occasions when it seemed to me that even a few minutes might be too long from the patient's point of view; there were other times when it seemed necessary to stay almost indefinitely, or at least open-endedly. And a decision as to how long to stay often required instant judgment.

I can remember times when I knew I was not welcome, and it takes effort to face the sense of failure which such knowledge brings. Having to come away from a bedside aware that one has been unable to help someone when perhaps they most needed help is painful. But that sense of failure counts for nothing, I believe, compared with the necessity of respecting the person's privacy. From our own life experience most of us have a good idea of just how sacred our own space is, and to approach someone who is sick, no matter in what role – and all the more so if I am there in the role of a pastoral carer – is only acceptable if that person indicates to me in some way or other that I am welcome. The only thing that matters must surely be the wish of the patient.

And after the ability to judge a situation and to know whether to go or to stay, I believe that the next most important sense a pastoral carer in a hospital needs is the ability to listen. Somewhere I read, 'Contemplative listening is a form of kenosis and, in the long run, the path to unconditional love.' This seems to me to cover much about this ministry, and especially in a hospital setting. (Indeed, it has struck me too that it could also be usefully said about love and friendship.)

The fact is that what most people long for in life is for someone to listen to their story without interruption and without judgment. No doubt this is why the role of the counsellor has become so important in so many people's lives today, and the need for highly trained personnel in pastoral care is very obvious.

But it takes time, and lots of it, to learn how to listen properly. In the fast-moving world of today anyone wishing to enter the ministry of pastoral care needs to acquire highly trained listening skills.

It even takes time to learn how not to run away! It can be difficult to listen to the woes of an elderly person, or to someone who is ill. It can take enormous effort to stay put. Sometimes I think this is because we are at one remove from the story and therefore it doesn't touch us at our core. Yet if we wish to minister to people at this level then we must learn to be touched – in fact, we need to feel the pain of the narrator.

And in order to be able to tune into another's pain we need first of all to be able to accept our own. As human beings, we will all have experienced spiritual pain at some time in our lives, it's part of the human condition. The acceptance of our own pain is the first step towards being able to empathise with the pain of another.

It was the extraordinary ability of Jesus to feel compassion for others that marked out his life and mission. Those who knew him have left us a record. I have already written of his encounter with the woman at the well, and there are many more such stories in which his compassion is manifest: that of the raising of the widow's son at Nain (Lk: 7:11-18); of Jairus's daughter (Lk: 8); of the haemorrhaging woman (Lk: 8:43-48), to name but a few. His ministry to those who were suffering can be seen clearly in the accounts of his public life which have been left to us.

As I see it, anyone who enters into the ministry of pastoral care takes on in a very specific way the role of Christ. It may well be that on any particular day a pastoral carer may be the only person the other will encounter and therefore the only one with the opportunity to be Christ to that other. It is a daunting thought, and yet it seems to me to be the truth.

And as I see it, two things are necessary in order for someone to prepare to enter into such a role. The first is prayer. A constant recollecting that God is with us in all our human frailty will, I believe, help us through the difficulties that are daily faced by anyone taking on this extraordinary ministry.

The second, I believe, is an awareness that even in the most difficult circumstances ministry is almost always reciprocal. In my time in pastoral care I discovered very quickly that I was being ministered to by those patients whom I visited; by a look or a word or a touch they very quickly demonstrated their compassion for me.

I once read something written by a theologian about our encounters with one another: he said that it was his belief that any meeting between two people – provided, of course, that that meeting is not deliberately violent or destructive – has the potential to be sacramental. In other words, as I understand him, the Spirit uses us, in our dealings with each other, as instruments for the flowing to and fro of grace. And I find this a marvellous idea because it puts us in the position of being able to do as St Paul suggests we do, that is, to 'pray always'. I am convinced that with a reliance on prayer and an awareness of the reciprocity of ministry it is possible for someone to undertake this exacting role.

To finish, since I have dared to write on this ministry, I will dare to end on a note of caution: I recently heard on good authority that it is believed that there will soon be a dearth of trained hospital pastoral carers in Ireland – presumably because of the dearth of religious vocations in general. If this be true, I sincerely hope that the powers-that-be in the Christian churches – and especially in my own church – will take the necessary steps *now* to ensure that enough personnel are trained in this essential ministry. Leaving such matters to chance and/or to be filled by untrained personnel – no matter how well-intentioned – will, as I see it, be a failure to respond in an adequate way to the most vulnerable in our society. And if we fail to respond to the most vulnerable, then I suspect we do not have the right to call ourselves Christians.

PART TWO

The Wider Picture

Conversation

The owner of the guesthouse pointed out a part of the stone wall which dipped slightly and said, 'If you climb over that, and then walk along the track between those two poles over there, and through the next field, you'll come to a beautiful little beach, and I'll guarantee you'll have it all to yourself, all day.'

I did as he said. I was accompanied by a small dog and when we entered the second field we were met by two ponies who fell into line behind us. We all then processed solemnly on and it struck me that we must have made some sight.

On arrival at the sand dunes the ponies gave up and when I got to the beach itself the dog went home also – duty done, perhaps.

I looked around me. I was in a tiny cove, with rocks to my right and left and, in between, a beautiful little bay of golden sand. It was a pet day with the water shimmering and sparkling in the sun. Far in the distance I could see the twin spires of Clifden and, to my right, the mountains. And there wasn't another living soul in sight. Bliss.

I took out a book but the water looked so inviting that I felt I had to try it out. I wasn't really swimming, just allowing myself to be carried back and forth by the in-coming waves. If there's a better way of relaxing. I haven't yet found it.

And then the sleek head apeared, and it seemed to me that the seal was at most only about twelve yards from me. He was looking straight at me, and I looked back. Was I intruding, I wondered? I kept very quiet, barely moving. So did he. And I have no idea just how long we gazed at each other, sizing one another up.

Eventually I moved to go back to the shore. The seal disappeared from sight. But as I stepped into the shallow water, lo and behold! up came his head again, almost exactly where I had been a few moments earlier.

I stood still and he disappeared, only to re-appear a moment or two later, a little further out.

I realised then that I was being coaxed back into the water; this was a game.

Quietly I waded in again, and treaded water again. So did he. And all the while we watched each other. Again the time went by, I don't know how much time. Only when I began to feel cold did I dare to break away, standing upright and walking through the shallow water back towards the beach.

But I wasn't allowed to go yet; the game apparently wasn't yet over. I glanced back and there he was, almost at my side. I stood and pondered. How was I going to bring this breath-taking conversation to an close?

I was by now feeling quite cold, so I came out of the water and dried myself down. And all the while I was under surviellance from only a few yards away.

Eventually, as a compromise, I gather my belongings and moved out on to the point of the rocks which protruded into the sea. This meant that the seal could swim in near to me, and we could still be within easy communication.

And there I spent the next couple of hours, reading, writing and soaking up the sun. And all the while my incredible friend kept me close company, his beautiful head never more than a couple of yards from where I sat. Very occasionally he would disappear for a short time but invariably he would be back, almost within arm's length, and we would resume our silent communing. It was, I felt, an extraordinary encounter, by any standards.

Much later on in the day, as I made my way back to the guesthouse, I reflected on just how wrong my host had been: by no stretch of the imagination had I spent the day on my own. Far from it.

And, as a result, I was certainly the richer.

In my element

It was one of those days in which I seemed to be idle, yet restless. I had tried reading but lacked any real concentration; I had tried answering letters, but there was no flow. And so I found myself, against my better judgement, picking up the remote control and zapping. Even as I did so I wished I had had the good sense to look up the programmes in advance, but it was too late for that.

And then I heard the familiar voice, and as I listened the picture on the screen became clear, revealing the smiling, crinkled-up eyes of Seamus Heaney. I had had the great good fortune to stumble upon a BBC programme which had been especially made to celebrate the poet's sixtieth birthday, and it was only a matter of seconds before I became enthralled.

Interspersed with contemporary footage, the film comprised snippets from documentaries which Heaney himself had made when a young man. I had never seen any of them before. And they were wonderful pieces, evocative and captivating; films of land- and sea-scapes; of bogs and trees; of wind and rain. And throughout the showing of them Heaney read from his own writings, speaking as only he can of the places where he had filmed – to him, holy places. I realised I was in for a feast.

At one point he stood in a soggy bog and explained in great detail how through millennia of growth and decay the bog had evolved and of how, because of its evolving, it had been possible for us as a people to survive, throughout many thousands of years, right up to today, enduring all types of hardships and hazards. And then he said that because the bog itself had actually helped us to survive, it had shaped us and was in fact part and parcel of the very stuff of which we are made.

And this, he said, quite literally means that for us to stand in such a bog today means that we are 'standing in our element'.

When the programme was over I went to the dictionary and looked up the word 'element'. The definition was 'component part; unanalysable substance'.

And it was thus that I came to understand better than I had ever understood before just why we use the expression 'in my element' when we want to describe an experience of great joy, or of a really powerful sense of well-being. (I hope that anyone reading this will know what I am talking about – I hope you will at some point or points in your life have felt this sense of well-being also.)

And I think that different people experience it in different circumstances: some may know it through physical activity such as running; others perhaps through music; some – and I count myself among this group – in the cut and thrust of a one-to-one tussle of words with someone of like mind. For me, there's nothing which makes me feel so alive as a good encounter with a loved sparring partner.

And I think that I experience this when I am totally engaged – when I feel that I am part of something from which I cannot be separated; that 'unanalysable component' which is a part of my very essence.

And, as I see it, it's only a small step from that point to believing that one day, in some as yet unimagined way, I will, ultimately and finally, be 'in my element'. And it is towards this belief that I try to move in hope.

The stuff of rock

I am always drawn to the Céide Fields. They fascinate me, and I find them magnetic. I'm drawn to the collapsed stone walls, shining white in the bog. I'm drawn to the turf in which those stone walls are embedded, that same turf which has bleached them of all colour over thousands of years, leaving them gleaming white like old bones bleached by the sun; and I'm drawn also to the sheer immensity of the as yet uncovered parts of the settlement, as I wonder, as so many others do, what secrets still lie hidden in this magical place.

I love the Interpretative Centre itself, with its life-sized figures depicting the lives of the people of long ago. But even more than all of these things, I am drawn to the history of the actual formation of the ground itself and, most of all, of the cliffs nearby.

The cliffs at the Céide Fields are at once magnificent and terrifying. When you look down at them from the viewing place above you can see the sea birds miles below, circling round and round before alighting on their nests which are so incredibly built into the cliff face. Each component to me seems a miracle in itself.

And yet, despite the awe they inspire in me, I know of no other place where I feel so at home with the elements. Grey or sunny, the air still or with a wild wind whipping round me, wet or dry, I'm happy when I am standing or sitting near this holy ground.

The last time I was there I spoke to a very courteous young man who was working there for the summer and I asked him if he would show me on my map just exactly where the Carrowmore Tombs were, on the road between Ballina and Sligo. I had failed to find them on my way out. Obligingly, he

marked the spot and also explained to me in detail just how I
would be sure to see them on my return journey.

And then I made a mistake. It wasn't intentional, I was really
just making polite conversation, but I should have thought it
through. I said to this local Mayoman that I had heard that there
was a megalithic site in Sligo which is believed to be even older
than the Céide Fields.

He drew himself up to his full height, perhaps five feet ten or
eleven – at any rate he had the edge on me – and, looking down
most sternly at me he said, 'Wait, now! We haven't finished dig-
ging here yet; you never know what might yet be found here.
We're not giving in without a fight, that's for sure! We could still
have the oldest known site on this island!'

I muttered lamely that I had meant no harm, but it was plain
to see that I had touched a raw nerve. However, with inate cour-
tesy he smiled at me and then bowed – an acceptance of my apol-
ogy. I suspect, too, that he was making excuses for me because he
pitied me, coming as I do from the Pale.

After we parted I went back to the cliffs once more. And then
it came to me: sure, this young man was part and parcel of these
cliffs – majestic, proud, stern, and, like the cliffs, made of rock. It
struck me that if you happened to have him on your side, you
would probably be all right for life. I recalled his straight young
shoulders, his upright frame, his dark hair and even darker eyes
– and suddenly I recognised all of the men which Sean Keating
has depicted in his paintings, West of Ireland men, tall, proud,
strong, sternly gazing out at us from the canvasses. And I realised
that these men were portrayed by the artist in this fashion because this is precisely what they are: part and parcel of the very
rock on which I was standing. Tough? perhaps; unyielding?
maybe so. But also unshakable, and therefore completely reli-
able; of the very same stuff as this piece of earth in this remote
corner of our island.

And at least for those few moments I seemed to understand
clearly how we can be shaped by the very ground on which we
live. It was a revelatory moment.

Difference

It seems to me, looking at the stem of most flowers when they are in bloom, that almost always the stem curves gently and graciously, the weight of the head of the flower dictating the curve and, of course, each stem being the perfect match for the weight which it must bear. It would I think be hard to imagine anything more subtle than this curved line in, say, the stem of a daisy or of a primrose.

Not so, however, with the buttercup. The buttercup is astonishing for more than its colour; it is astonishing also because of the structure of its stem. Its stem is completely straight and not only that, but where it divides in two the angle at the dividing point is absolutely sharp, as sharp as any angle on an architect's drawing.

And I am enchanted by this. The lines are so clean, so precise, so unlike the stems of almost all other flowers that they seem to defy all the usual laws of nature. See for yourself, when you next have the chance.

This, then, as I see it, is the shape and story of the buttercup.

That is, except on the banks of the River Boyne. For some reason unfathomable to me, on the banks of the Boyne the buttercups are different; their foliage is different, and their stems have no angles. They curve gently, like the stems of all other flowers. And I am completely baffled by this difference.

When I see them, therefore, I find myself caught into a prayer that I will continue to be baffled with surprise and joy.

But, even more, I pray that I may learn to discern just when to bend gently with life, like the stems of most flowers, and when to set off at my own unique angle.

Journeying

I knew in my heart and soul that if I didn't make an effort the year would pass without my seeing a cowslip or hearing a cuckoo. Living in a city, it was unlikely that it would happen in my back yard. So I made the journey to the Céide Fields in North Mayo – that extraordinary discovery of the abodes of ancestors which is, they say, a thousand years older than Newgrange.

I found a friendly house at the foot of Nephin and I stayed there three days. And each morning I heard the cuckoo, and lining the roads round about I came upon myriads of strong, full cowslips; and these two rewards for my journey I stored in my memory as food for the rest of my urban year.

Two other incidences which occurred at that time stand out: the first was that when I told the lady of the house that I was heading for the Céide Fields she said, 'Well, there'll be no cobwebs left around your heart after that visit!' And of course she was right; the magnificent terrifying grandeur of the cliffs, the force of the wind, the wonder of the five thousand year old stone walls of the Fields took away my everyday irritations. I stood on the cliff edge and watched the sea birds far below me, and my obsessions vanished.

The second thing which rested with me was this: as our young guide was explaining to a group of us how the Fields were laid out she said 'No one really knows why this once densely populated area, where farmers had lived and kept their herds for centuries, came to be deserted. Perhaps it was over-grazing.' And she bent down, picked up a handful of clay, rubbed it between her hands and said with what I thought was wonderful authority, 'That's how it feels to me, anyway. Over-grazing. The soil is dead. There's no life left in it'.

Foolishly, I bent down and picked up a handful of clay, copying her movements by rubbing it in my hands; and as I did so I realised with a shock that nothing in my life's experience gave me the knowledge that this young person had, by which I could with any authority judge the life, or lack of life, in the soil.

At that moment I envied her, but I was also re-affirmed that the idea that I should make the journey was indeed necessary, if only to remind myself of how in the interests of supposedly convenient city living we are often greviously impoverished.

It seems to me that there are times when we must look for our Creator; otherwise we might forget.

Fun and games

A theologian told me this story:

A friend of his, another theologian, was walking on a beach when it began to rain. He crawled under an upturned boat for shelter and after a while, when his eyes became accustomed to the dark, he became aware that a pair of bright eyes stared at him. When his eyes had become more accustomed to his surroundings he saw that he was sharing the shelter with a small fox cub. They stared at one another until the rain stopped, and then the cub left first.

When the man crawled out he found that the cub was waiting for him; it was crouched down on its front paws, and its tail stuck up in the air. As soon as the man appeared, the cub jumped towards him, and then away again, taking up the same playful position. So, the man took a small jump towards the cub, and then jumped back. And the cub did likewise. And for the next ten minutes they played thus, back and forth, parry and thrust, both of them apparently oblivious to everything else around them.

But then the man took stock. 'What', he wondered, 'if someone were to see me? They'll think I've gone mad.' And for a moment he almost stopped the game. But another thought superceded the first, and it was that he wasn't mad at all, but was simply responding to creation in the most spontaneous way possible. And it struck him that any lesser response would have been a failure on his part to enter into the full Mystery.

I love this story. It calls to mind for me the marvellous sense of fun that must permeate the Creator, and this in turn results for us in moments of sheer joy. Such stories are not nonsense; rather, they are the very essence of truth.

Surprise

I turned from a noisy main road into a quiet one on a lovely sunny morning and the road on which I now found myself was a very wide one, with an unusually expansive skyline for an urban place.

Because it was so bright, the moving shadow coming towards me was very noticable. I looked up, and just above me were two great swans. Now they were so near that I could hear the slow, rhythmic beating of their massive wings and I watched enthralled as, with necks fully stretched, they made their elegant journey, barely higher than the roof-tops. I presumed that they were heading for the canal, which was only a mile or so away; and I had no idea at all from whence they had come. It was clear that nothing was going to cause them to deviate from their path, nor could anyone or anything have undertaken a journey with more purpose and grace.

I compared my own journey that morning: almost motionless traffic, human made, and no-one getting anywhere. And I envied these enormous, elegant birds as they enjoyed the freedom that was theirs.

The two swans lifted my heart and coloured my day, and they also reminded me of something I had heard someone say concerning the fullness and immediacy of grace. He had said, 'Forgiveness is all around us, manifested everywhere, if we will only look; it is in the beauty that surrounds us and which can so suddenly take us by surprise and joy'. And then he added, 'Forgiveness *is* the very air we breathe'. I believe he is right.

Gift

I had traversed the country from east to west, seeking a breath of air away from city activity. I only stopped when I reached a friendly house facing the Atlantic and, although it was almost dark, I could just make out the shape of the Reek behind me and glimpse Clew Bay in front of me. The silence of the night was all-enveloping.

In such a place it's virtually impossible to run away from oneself – there's nothing to hide behind.

Next morning I opened the door first thing, the better to experience this awakening, so different to that of a city awakening. It was a grey morning, soft and mild, and still there was the wonderful lack of noise, as if to prove to me straight away that places and moments of peace do, indeed, exist.

And then I saw them coming towards me. Not one, not two, as I might have seen on the Dodder in Dublin, but five herons, languidly making their way across the tree-tops in front of me, the gentle shape of each pair of enormous wings seeming to lazily write a soft letter 'm' repeatedly across the broad canvas of the sky. Their trailing legs stretched out behind them and there was a wonderful sense of a complete lack of the need for hurry, for anyone, anywhere.

Five! The sheer extravagance of it took my breath away. My eyes followed them until they were out of sight, lost against the grey of the Reek.

Who would not have felt blessed just then?

Later in the day I stopped a young man to ask directions, because I was in a part of the country with which I am not very familiar.

I asked 'If I go a bit further along this road, will I find a beach to walk along?'

Without hesitation he answered me: 'Oh, you'll find a beach all right, but as to getting a walk, well, I can't promise you that because what with the high tide, the autumn equinox, the full moon and the wind coming from the west, you'll be very lucky indeed if there's any bit of beach left to walk along.'

This was surely an answer which I felt I could never have got from a city dweller. And not for the first time I realised that those of us who choose to live 'conveniently close to our work' often do so at great cost to ourselves.

Mystery

The stream running through the sand was too wide to leap over and too deep to go through in our shoes, but we wanted to walk out as far as we could just to get a sense of the space, so we took off our shoes and waded through the water.

And it turned out to be well worth it, because I believe we walked for the best part of a mile without reaching the edge of the sea. In fact, it almost looked as if we could have kept going till we reached America. There were one or two tiny fishing boats out on the horizon and earlier we had passed a few families pic-nicking in the sandhills, but even though we knew of the existence of these other people the surrounding space was so vast that it really felt as if there were only the two of us inhabiting the world at that particular moment. And we could feel the heat of the sun on our backs, while a warm breeze blew in our faces. Bliss.

I picked up a stone from the beach and examined it carefully. This particular one was very smooth, and quite heavy; and it was a grey/blue colour, with stripes running through it.

And then I picked up another. This one was surprisingly light, and it was a sort of mottled brown, and completely differ-ent from the first. They were different in colour, shape, size, and texture. And yet each was beautiful and, as stones, were perfect.

I thought about this for a while, and realised that they were in fact incomparable, just as any two people are incomparable.

I sat on a rock and stared at the two stones, and then I began to wonder about their history – their very origins, in fact. And it struck me that I myself was very young, because these two stones which I was holding, and the myriad others lying round about me on the sand, were all infinitely older than I; it almost seemed

that they had been around for ever. And I also realised with a
sense of awe that when I and my progeny have all gone, these
stones will endure, and others will pick them up, perhaps, in
other places, and wonder.

And this set up a train of questions within me: why are they
made of sterner stuff than I? Why am I so much more vulnerable
than they? What is their purpose? What is my purpose? And,
perhaps above all: from whence did they, from whence did I and
everyone else come? It struck me that there were more questions
in my head than there were stones on the beach.

But the question which seemed most fitting for me to pose to
myself at that moment was this: How can I possibly hold even
the simplest object, even a stone, in my hand, and not be pro-
foundly drawn into the Total Mystery?

What we need, I think, is to make the time, or take the time, to
look at such an object. And if we will only do this every now and
then, perhaps many of our doubts would melt away, and our
fears become groundless.

The Esker Ridge

The Esker Ridge is a fault line which, roughly speaking, runs across the centre of Ireland in a line between Galway and Dublin. It is a continuous rise in the ground, and is made up of stone, gravel and boulders. It is not arable land.

I have been fascinated by it for most of my life, ever since learning geography through Irish in school, I heard its Irish name, *Eiscir Riada*. From then on, whenever I crossed the country I used to watch out for it, catching glimpses of it at different points along the side of the road between Dublin and Galway. I think it became even clearer when the new, wider roads were opened up.

Sometimes I find that city people don't know about it. They think I made it up, and some have even got indignant with me when I exclaim out loud as we bowl along; I have suddenly spotted the fact that we are passing close to, or through, the Esker.

Within the last few years I have had two new surprises about this marvellous Ridge. In the first place, I heard about a retreat house where one could retire for a few days to have a quiet time, and when I went there I found that my little chalet was actually perched on top of the Ridge. I was delighted!

The second surprise was much more dramatic. Reading Tim Robinson's *Setting Foot on the shores of Connemara*, I read, for the first time I believe, that Ireland and England did not, as I had always assumed, break away in one piece from mainland Europe all those millions of years ago. Robinson, by way of explaining how the stones of Connemara differ so completely from the slab rock of the Burren and the Aran Islands, states that billions of years ago the top half of Ireland was separate from the bottom half by an ocean – called Japetus by geologists, he says – and that when the two continents north and south of this ocean eventually collided, 'squeezing Japetus out of geography,' the island of Ireland was formed; the Esker Ridge is the joining line. I am as excited by this discovery as if I were the first to hear of it! Somehow or other, events of this magnitude help me to keep things in perspective.

And not least do I ask myself: who organised all of this? No mere man or woman, that's for sure. And I wonder anew at the fickleness of my faith.

Trust

By any standards it had been a wet week in west Cork. Perched in a little cottage high on the top of Sheep's Head, the only living creatures around apart from ourselves seemed to be the sheep themselves, one large and one very small rabbit, and the birds. But it's fair to say also that now and then a shaft of sunlight would manage to break through the clouds and when it did we revelled in the glory. At other times we were completely shrouded in mist. This was certainly the way to forget about rush-hour traffic, and that was the whole purpose of the exercise.

Perhaps because of all the rain, or maybe because everyone was tired on arrival, we were not the least bit sociable. And it was therefore not until the very day of our departure that we dropped by to say hello to Agnes, our nearest neighbour.

Lucky for us that we did, because it was then that we met the fox. He was only a few months old. Agnes had found him outside her cottage one day, cold and hungry and, assuming that his mother had either been killed or had abandoned him, she immediately adopted him. And he her.

While she told this story to us the fox sat beside us. The neatest thing imaginable, he sat with his ears pricked up, listening as if to make sure the story was told correctly. His front paws were placed together as impeccably as a cat's; his feline eyes – and I never knew till that moment that foxes have feline eyes – looked back at us with great friendliness and interest, and his white front gleamed against the rusty red of the rest of his coat. He took a photocall like a film star. And we, the city slickers, were mesmerised.

It's fair to say that the memory of that encounter with such a magnificent creature has helped to sustain a number of us through the chaos and noise of city living.

The Stack

The Stack, or Dún Briste, that massive piece of land broken off from the cliffs of North Mayo and standing proud and solitary in the fierce Atlantic Ocean, fascinates me more every time I see it. It's like an open book, each layer a different page, if only we knew how to read it. And it stands there, open and inviting, for all of us. I find it irresistible.

I'm no geologist – I wish I were – but I love this mass of rock. It's a great place for a good think.

If I lie flat on the headland and look across at The Stack, things seem to fall into perspective. Huge as it is, it fits into the sea, sky, and landscape around it – and I myself become small beyond measure. It's almost impossible to fathom the ages which have passed since it first broke off from the mainland, more difficult still to imagine the age of those invisible layers lying below the sea line. Our lives are only split seconds in comparison.

And yet even as I look at its huge bulk I know that some day the merciless pounding of the sea will bring it down; nothing material on this earth is constant.

Everyday living can prevent us from thinking about these things. Crises, small or large, engulf us. Yet the wise ones tell us it's good to ponder the wider scale of things, and I for one believe them. And that's why I return, whenever I get the chance, to be renewed and restored by that extraordinary mass of rock which aeons ago became severed from the Mayo coast.

The Big Bang

Sometimes when I'm away on holidays I purchase a string of coloured stones or beads and take them home and then I re-thread them into a necklace, for myself or someone else. These are inexpensive, not precious stones, but I love the variety, even in texture, which can be found in just one such string, and I love matching them up, grading them according to their various shadings, sizes and shapes. It can be exacting work, and sometimes hard on the hand and arm and should be taken on in small doses, but to me the joy of seeing their remarkable colours and shapes outweighs the problems which sometimes manifest themselves in the working of them.

Recently I found some lovely green/pink stones. In fact, they were unrefined chips of tourmaline which, had they been of higher quality, might have had some little value, but this was not so. I was examining them in detail when I chanced on one, smaller than half the size of my small finger nail, and I noticed that there was a 'flaw' in its centre, a black spot, right inside the stone. On closer examination I realised that from this black spot there appeared to emanate a tiny shower of smaller specks, almost like a sun-burst, or like a still from a shot on television of some vast explosion.

I brought the stone to someone who knows about these things and enquired of him as to what this flaw might be, and how it might have come about. He examined it minutely and then he said, 'Yes, it's a flaw all right, but it's a "natural" flaw; that is it hasn't happened recently. Something exploded within this piece of stone aeons ago; in fact, it may well have happened at the time of the Big Bang.' And he grinned, and handed the stone back to me.

I came home with the precious treasure tightly held in my hand. Imagine! Here I had a mirror-image, in microcosm, of the moment when everything had started! I could hardly believe it! Within this tiny piece of matter was a record of the beginning of all time, the start of everything. And but for that beginning, nothing would be, including ourselves.

It strikes me that there must be millions of such stones. Once, years ago, two of my children and myself found a grey stone on Killiney beach which had a most extraordinary marking within it which I now think must have been caused by an explosion; could it have happened at another time, or at that same time, when everything began?

And then I remembered that not long ago I attended a lecture given by a physicist and, ignorant as I am on all matters scientific, nevertheless I'm almost sure that I heard him say, 'Aeons ago, in the course of about four seconds, something happened. And since then, nothing much has happened at all.'

It makes you think.

Jumping for Joy

All the lambs in the field had black faces, which seemed to make them even more appealing. There were dozens of them, and a fair number of mothers also. But it wasn't feeding time, so the mothers were having a peaceful few minutes.

The lambs were behaving like children; there was a beautiful beech tree nearby and for some reason many of its roots were exposed. And the lambs were actually scrambling up over the roots and it seemed as if each of them, like any child, wanted to be King – or Queen – of the castle. So they took it in turns to butt each other off the top root, in order to enjoy a few moments' glory before they in turn were unceremoniously dethroned.

A few weren't interested in this game. They stayed in the middle of the field and every now and then one of them would jump sky-high although, as my companion remarked, there was nothing there to jump. And he added that they reminded him of women at an airport who jump up and down while waiting for their loved ones even before those loved ones come into sight.

I love this picture of ordinary people being so moved by joy that it manifests itself in their wanting to jump in the air. And I try to remember that, when I am in the middle of a day in which I feel the very opposite. If I can remember just such an occasion it reminds me that, despite what I may be feeling on this particular day, there is a very real chance that on another day, and hopefully not too far into the future, I will know joy again.

Learning to wait

It's a fair few years ago now, and all I know is that we were on the north side of Killary Harbour – I wish I could be more specific, but I wasn't on familiar territory There was a full car load of us, and we ranged in age through about 60 years, the youngest being about four. We had all the necessary trappings for a really good picnic, and when we saw another car and a tractor safely driving across the strand and up a steep track on the other side we followed suit. And then they disappeared into a farmyard and we had the headland to ourselves. The sun was splitting the rocks and it was by any standards a pet day.

The picnic was a great success and afterwards there was little or no activity because of the heat. Everyone seemed content just to laze quietly in the sun. And I remember being suddenly aware that it was nothing short of a miracle that everyone was so content because some months earlier we had had a bereavement of great moment to us all; we had lost the head of the family, the very one who would himself have been the organiser of just such an outing as this. And when I remembered our great sorrow and grief at that time it was indeed a miracle that we could enjoy such a day again, without him. Yet this is how it was, and even those who had been most affected by his death could laugh and smile. It was indeed miraculous.

And then a small child took a wander on her own, never out of sight, and coming back some minutes later she said in a most matter-of-fact voice, 'There's now no way we can go home, not till the tide goes out.'

We all scrambled to our feet to see what she was talking about and sure enough the tide was fully covering every inch of the strand we had driven over, and covering it at some depth.

There was nothing for it, then, but to dig in, for about five hours. Happily, in the glorious weather, it was no hardship to any of us. It was simply a question of waiting.

Some years later I happened on a small piece written by Henri Neuwen, called 'A Spirituality of Waiting'. Almost immediately, although I hadn't thought of it for years, the picnic at Killary Harbour sprang into my mind. And I think the reason was because we had had to wait: to wait for the tide to recede, to wait for the sorrow of bereavement to soften gently and pull back from us. And both had indeed happened, but not through any action of ours. Ours had been the passive part.

There are times when waiting isn't easy, that's for sure. But there are also times, in so far as I can understand these things, when it seems that to wait is all that is asked of us.

Belief

In my childhood I felt a sense of wonder about what seemed to me the irony of the fact that some inanimate things live so much longer than we humans do. And yet we would always purport to hold that a person is of much greater value than any object. I remember that when I was young I used to stare at a large wardrobe in our house and wonder just how many people had used it before I was born, and how many would use it after I was gone. And what struck me most forcibly was the apparent solidity of the wardrobe, and the total and very visible fragility of our human bodies – and God knows we are daily reminded of this fragility just by reading the newspapers today, when everything seems to depend on travelling at speed.

Over time I came to realise that it is this very fragility in living things which makes it imperative that we try in every way we can to protect them – and not just ourselves but everything that breathes and which could in one fell swoop be so easily obliterated: plants, trees, animals, ourselves. A blast of wind, a crushing blow, and it can all be over. The vulnerability of living things, ourselves included, is very real.

And yet, and yet? ... Are there not times also when, even if only for a split second, we are suddenly aware that there is more to us than this fragility? Are there not moments, of pure joy, perhaps, or of love, when we sense a never-ending-ness in ourselves? The psychologists would have us remember that 'I am more than my flesh; more than my thoughts; more than my feelings'. They are pointing out that there is something else in us all, an essence, which is indeed indestructible.

If I can remind myself of this, then I find that it is possible, at least at times, for me to hope – and sometimes believe – that this very part is a part of the Source from whence all of creation comes, the part which links everyone and everything together.

In the good times it is sometimes not too difficult to believe that there is something in us which will endure, held in being, held in love.

And in the bad, I try to hang on to hope.

Best self

A friend of mine told me recently that when she was at school an enlightened nun used to say to her class, 'Be your best selves.'

It seems a remarkable statement to have been made in the fifties; in many ways I feel that to be ourselves in those days was to incur all sorts of wrath.

But thinking about it now it would seem to be the best lesson we could have learnt. And even if some of us are only learning it late in life, better late than never.

It often strikes me as amazing that we humans are the only creatures who can deviate from being our best selves. To plants, animals, all other living things, it is utterly natural; they are born, they grow, they bloom, and then they die. If I examine a daisy I will see its perfection; if I take the time to watch a rose unfold, change colour, and let off its exquisite perfume over some hours, I am watching perfection. If I watch the cat slowly insinuate himself over the garden fence and then stretch out in the sun on an impossibly narrow ridge on top of the coalshed, I am watching the most complex series of individual and collective movements done to perfection and with consummate ease. Almost effortlessly, because of what he is – and he can only be his best self – the cat will achieve his desire – to bask in the heat of the sun unperturbed.

We are the only living creatures who can make a mess of things, because we are conscious beings. Hence we have responsibilities. And hence, it would seem to me, we have to do some unlearning.

I listened to a lecture recently, and I was struck in particular by one thing the speaker said. He said, 'You will not be asked [at the point of death] why you were not more like Jesus Christ throughout your life; you will be asked why you were not more like yourself.'

A salutary thought. And, allowing for his belief, and for all we have learned and try to believe for ourselves, and if there is truth in any of it, then I think that the idea of trying to be our best selves is as good as we'll get.

It may take some doing. Many of us, I believe, have layers and layers, of 'public persona', or 'false self' to peel away, before we reach the kernel of who we really are. And the peeling can be painful in the extreme. I wonder sometimes about that pain and just why it is so acute and I think the answer may be that we are afraid that if we keep peeling we may just find that, like an onion, there is no kernel …

Perhaps one of the bonuses of reaching mature years is that the risk of this peeling away becomes more attractive. There is less time to worry about peripheral things and there is a pull towards truth. Stevie Smith says, in her poem 'Pad, Pad':

What I cannot remember is how I felt when you were unkind
All I know is, if you were unkind now I should not mind.
Ah me, the power to feel exaggerated, angry and sad
The years have taken from me. Softly I go now, pad pad.

I find these few lines very restful!

Searches for the truth: Ways of Prayer?

I never cease to be amazed at how often, even in a group of people where religion would not be the perceived common interest, a lively discussion will come about on that very subject.

Recently I found myself in just such a group. How the subject of theology came about I don't know, but suddenly someone present lobbed in the sentence: 'Theology is a luxury.' And that was debated with great vivacity. It was agreed that indeed so it was; when one remembers the innumerable people throughout the world whose only concern has to be their own and their loved ones' survival, then to have the time and energy to debate the finer theological points must surely be seen to be a luxury.

However, someone else quickly added, 'But it's a necessary luxury.' And that, too, was quickly agreed on by a number of the people present. For surely it is true that for those who know where the next meal is coming from, then *a fortiori* there is an obligation to think, to search, to discuss. Of course for many it is also a joy, bringing as it does a quickening, a vitality, to life. And, after all, is it not the ability to search for the truth that marks humankind out from the rest of creation? We *must* seek, we *must* ask questions; it is of our essence so to do.

These two views of theology, that it is both a luxury and a necessity, reminded me of something I heard a distinguished theologian say years ago: 'Anyone who thinks is a theologian.' I could see his point then and I can see it now. The only thing I might add is that perhaps most people are *students* of theology, rather than fully-fledged theologians, since the learning in this sphere can never be complete.

The discussion also recalled to my mind an earlier discourse, when a hard-pressed young mother of a large family once re-marked at a prayer meeting that her prayer had to be the peeling of the potatoes or the washing of the child or whatever domestic chore immediately occupied her. Another person present ex-pressed astonishment saying, 'I can't see any connection at all between peeling potatoes and prayer.' I, being more in tune with the experience of the first woman at that time, was in turn aston-ished that the second woman couldn't see the connection, and I thought of the theology of Seamus Heaney's beautiful lines in his poem 'Clearances', in which he describes his mother and himself, when he was a very young child, peeling potatoes together at the sink.

And all of this brought me round to the implied question in the title of this chapter: what is prayer?

I sometimes think that there must be as many answers to that question as there are human beings, but one definition which I find very appealing is that of Miriam Pollard OP in her book, *Acceptance*. She says: 'Prayer is a determining to accept our situ-ation.' Here, perhaps, is the kernel.

And perhaps this definition also gives us the link between theology and prayer. According to *The New Dictionary of Theology*, published by Gill and MacMillan in 1987 – where the definition of theology runs to seventeen pages – there is one sen-tence in particular which caught my eye: 'Henceforward [after the Christ event, when God became man in Jesus Christ] theology cannot be disengaged from involvement in worldly affairs.' Substitute the word 'domestic' for 'worldly' and I believe that that brings the peeling of potatoes right into the realm of theology, as well as into the realm of prayer: to echo Miriam Pollard, it is the acceptance of the moment.

Of course, even our best efforts are feeble. 'We do not even know how to pray', says Paul, and the longer I live the more I feel he is right. We cannot know; we can only try.

For how can we know? How can we, creatures, do other than be in constant awe of that which created everything else? What is there for us to say, except to give praise and thanks?

And yet the need to pray can often be strong; when things go wrong, for ourselves or for someone we love; when things are right – when we are deeply moved by joy and/or delight about something; and at less extreme times also, when we find the time to be quiet, to sit and think – or maybe just to sit. 'Thou has made us for thyself oh Lord, and our hearts are restless until they rest in thee.' Something draws us on; we seek, and therefore if we are lucky, we may end up in searching discussion.

Elsewhere in this book I have mentioned the fifteenth-century icon 'Trinity' by Andrei Rublev, and recently I saw an exhibition of icons by Fearghal O'Farrell, in St Peter's Church in Phibsboro. In the accompanying brochure this iconographer states, 'The actual painting of an icon is a slow process and is in itself a prayer.' He also says, 'The icon is "written" not painted, "read" not just viewed.' What a wonderful way to be able to define one's work! And indeed it is easy to agree; the enormous care and love which goes into the writing of an icon is very visible and can be the inspiration for an effort at prayer.

Recently I stumbled upon another example of an art form which to me seemed to be the epitome of prayer. I was walking past an art gallery in the city of Bath when my eyes were arrested by the extraordinary vibrancy of colour emanating from a painting hanging in the middle of the window, so vibrant that I found myself drawn to stop and then to enter.

Inside, I found the walls festooned with many other paintings, all of them equally eye-catching. There were about two dozen, quite large in size – perhaps 16" by 24" or thereabouts – and in so far as I can now remember they all depicted figures of a woman, usually on her own, sometimes with another. The figures were very stylised but at the same time very beautiful, with long, delicate faces and limbs, and flowing gowns. In every painting she was smiling, or at the least looking tranquil. This woman – perhaps it was not always the same woman, although it looked so to me – was usually in the foreground of the painting, and very often she carried something in her arms, perhaps a huge bunch of sunflowers or poppies, or sheaves of wheat. In the background were scenes of mountains or fields. And such was the peace that seemed to emanate from the scenes that I found it an exhibition which really lifted my heart, even at first glance.

Curious, I read the leaflet containing details about the artist. She is a South African, Estienne Sheppard, who now lives in the south of England. And in her statement about herself and her work she says that she paints from a perspective of peace which she believes comes from her intimate 'relationship' with God through the Lord Jesus Christ. She also states that her objectives in her painting are 'to bring joy to the homes that receive them [the paintings] and to give God the glory for any success that comes her way.' And this exhibition, although only four days old when I came across it, was a sell-out.

Having read all this, and having taken in the overall impact of the paintings as a whole and their riot of colour, I began to study each one individually. The very first was of a woman carrying sunflowers. The second was somewhat different: a little smaller, the colours a little more subdued, the woman in the picture was standing holding a door open, and behind her, outside, the sun was rising with brilliance. I looked at the title; it was called 'Open door to life'. I stood for a moment to take it all in and then moved on.

In the next there were two women and they were greeting each other with a kiss. I looked at the title. It said, 'The good news'. I stepped back, startled, and looked again at the previous painting, of the woman holding open the door. And then I thought: these two paintings are depictions of The Annunciation and The Visitation. I was delighted, and moved on, taking care now to study each painting slowly, and then to read each title.

Many of the works had simple, one-word titles, such as 'Peace' or 'Tranquillity'. Some showed women in domestic scenes; there was a picture of a woman gathering eggs in a hay barn, and another of a woman sitting beside a lemon tree. But every now and then, interspersed amongst these more 'secular' paintings, I came across one which stopped me in my tracks. There was, for example, a painting of a shepherdess, complete with shepherd's crook. I looked at the title; it read, 'Feed my sheep'. Yet again, there was a painting of a woman carrying a light wooden cross on her shoulders, but she seemed at ease with it, showing no sign that it weighed her down. The title simply stated, 'John 14:6'. And I realised with delight that I was looking at the work of an artist for our time, who through her giftedness could share her belief that Christ's command that we be 'other Christs' to each other was spoken to all Christians, regardless of gender. By depicting an 'other Christ' as 'Christa', Christ in the feminine, this artist seemed to me to be speaking the truth as she sees it with great and unaffected clarity; it is, her paintings appear to say, the humanity of Jesus that matters, over and above gender.

In such vein was the whole exhibition. For my part, I realised that I had come across no ordinary collection, but a labour of love by an extraordinary woman whose work had become a prayer of great depth. For those of us who must normally make do with more prosaic ways of prayer, how marvellous for us when through such works we are, even occasionally, temporarily uplifted from the mundane into a time of quiet, reflective beauty.

This example of prayer about which I have written, the visual and visible prayer of an artist, is, of course only one, specific form, and I can see the value of other forms which prayer can take also. There is a time and place for communal prayer, as in liturgies; for private prayer of all kinds; for prayers of petition, of praise, of thanksgiving, of contrition; a time for the prayer of sacred music. I believe that all of these diverse ways are, in the end, simply different ways of acknowledging that there is Something, Someone, greater than ourselves, and our varying and various efforts at prayer are a manifestation of our creatureliness. Recently someone told me of the warm response with which the enactment of the story of the Samaritan Woman and Jesus was received in his parish and, indeed, of how pleased members of another parish were that the Passion story was narrated during the Easter ceremonies by members of the congregation. It would seem that there are times when some visual form of storytelling helps people to enter into a mindset of recollection, as a help to breaking off from the general noisiness of today's world.

This reminds me of the fact that at present, although still in its infancy, there is a scheme afoot by some citizens of Dublin to create a space in the heart of the city, in the busy Temple Bar area, where passers-by will be able to drop in for a few moments or longer and, as it were, draw breath. Although Christian in inspiration, it is hoped that people of all creeds and of none will find a welcome there and that it will afford those who so wish the opportunity to take time out in an atmosphere of peace and tranquillity. Perhaps the very act of entering into such a space could constitute a form of prayer, since it is in itself a way of being open to what some have described the Sacrament of the Present Moment. Such, anyway, are the aspirations behind this particular project.

But perhaps, at the last, the prayer of determining to accept our situation encompasses all other forms of prayer. It is Amen; so be it; Fiat. It is the prayer of Paul. It is the prayer of Mary. And it is the prayer of Jesus in Gethsemane when, even though every fibre of his being abhorred what was happening to him, he was prepared to go through with it. 'If it be possible take this chalice from me. Yet not my will, but yours.' Not only was he determined to accept his own cruel situation, but he was also accepting of his own human, frail, completely understandable abhorrence of that situation. Fiat.

Such acceptance may be all that is asked of us. On a few occasions when I was very frightened and unable, because of that fear, to think of a formal prayer, I have heard the words running round in my head, 'I am desperately afraid.' And then it has dawned on me that because at that moment this fear is the only truth for me, then these words are in fact the only authentic prayer possible for me at that moment. So be it.

I remember someone else explaining prayer to me thus: 'To pray is to be constantly aware.' It's a lovely definition. If we can be constantly aware of all that is going on in and around us, we are bound to be in awe of the exquisite complexities of which everything is made up, and this awe would seem to me to constitute prayer.

Yet another definition comes to my mind: once, I was at a conference and I was surprised to meet an eminent theologian there who was obviously part of the establishment in which the conference was being held, but I hadn't known that. After we had greeted each other I asked him what his role was in the house. To my astonishment he said 'I pour the tea', and he smiled, picked up an enormous teapot and poured me a cup.

This is, I think, echoed in the artist Chris Doris's description of the menial tasks he did while on the summit of Croagh Patrick, about which I have written elsewhere in this book. He says, 'The logistics of keeping things clean and ordered, cooking and washing, were rituals renewed with value. No longer chores impeding me from being elsewhere, they were vital moments, as latent with opportunity as any other.' To me, this seems a clear definition of prayer.

And it would seem to me also that silence is often a prayer. Nowhere was this more obvious to me than during my chaplaincy training. To visit someone who is very ill, perhaps dying, may not need any words, just a presence, and this presence may in itself be the only prayer necessary at a particular time.

During our training we were advised to 'listen to the music behind the words' of the other. Such listening constitutes prayer I believe, and perhaps one of the most authentic forms. But it is not easy to listen to the pain of another, even as a form of prayer.

Again, sometimes I think that to be alone and at peace is at times the best prayer. It is an acceptance of the situation. Being alone may give us the best chance of listening to what is in our hearts, and the space to move into a positive acceptance of the present moment.

In fact, it is in such precious moments that I have come to hope, but there are times when things do not seem so simple. A few years ago, at the beginning of Lent, at a particular time when praying, for me, seemed elusive, I wrote the following:

Heavenly Source, from whence everything comes;
every breath, every thought, every feeling;
every whim, every joy, every sorrow;
above all, every question:
When I was young, everything was black and white
and if I couldn't make out which of those colours it was
I could ask those whom I trusted,
and I was told, and I accepted,
and life was simple then.
Now, however, there are varying shades of grey,
myriad shades, about which I knew nothing as a child.
Now nothing is clear any more.
And I find myself full of questions.
When I was young I used to pray,
'I believe in you, I hope in you and I love you'.
Now I can only pray:
'I try to believe, I try to hope, and I try to love.
But above all, God, I ask you questions.'
And you, because you are my Maker,
understand my questioning.
You, because you have fashioned me as I am,
are not surprised, annoyed, dismayed, shocked or impatient
– even with my impatience.
And because it is you who have put those questions into me,
it is right that I question you.
If, however, in your infinite wisdom
you choose not to answer me,
then that, too, is right.
And I will continue my questioning prayer.
And you, because you are the Source
from whence all my questioning comes,
will understand.
Amen.

However, there are times when my prayer can be quite different. I am writing this on February 1st, the first day of Spring, and the Feast day of St Brigid. It looks like a spring day, it feels like a spring day – a day when, perhaps, it might just be relatively 'easy' to pray. I am reminded of something I once heard: 'Forgiveness is the air we breathe.' So it seems to me today. As the sun shines through the patchy clouds, as the blades of the daffodils begin to stretch themselves towards the light, as tiny buds show their presence on the still bare branches of the shrubs and trees, what I feel most of all is gratitude for 'this most amazing day' and, at least for these few moments, a certainty of the existence of a loving Source towards whom I try to move in hope.

On such a blessed day, then, it seems fitting that I should borrow a well-known and much loved Irish blessing to bring these random thoughts on prayer to a close:

Deep peace of the Running Wave to you.
Deep peace of the Flowing Air to you.
Deep peace of the Quiet Earth to you.
Deep peace of the Shining Stars to you.
Deep peace of the Son of Peace to you.
Amen.

In Memoriam: The Story of a Photograph

She wasn't well, but she felt that there were 'miles to go' before she could sleep; she wanted to visit certain places, most notably in the west of Ireland, where she had only been a couple of times in her busy life, and she felt that she would like to know them better. And so she embarked on an ambitious plan for the week's holiday, to cover as much ground as possible and make up for this lacuna.

First, then, to the Burren. There we walked over the flat plateaux of limestone rock, our scarves tied tightly round our wind-blown heads, rain beating down on us most of the time, and she taking photographs of the flora and fauna as we went. Very occasionally we were blessed by a shaft of sunlight, but almost immediately it would disappear as quickly as it had come, and we were left braving the inclement elements once more.

Then it was on up along the coast of Connemara, stopping to walk on a beach at Ballyconneely before proceeding to Leenane for a night, where the weather was kinder to us. And from thence to Westport, where Brigin and Stephen received us with such gentle hospitality.

Back, then, along the edge of Lough Mask, visiting Ballintubber Abbey on the way; through Cong and on to the shores of Lough Corrib, where we had booked into a wonderful B and B, crammed with enthusiastic French and German fishermen and women. Each evening was a delight, as they regaled each other about the near misses, the ones that got away, the extraordinary fights that had been lost and won at the end of lines.

And my companion – my sister Ann – loved every minute of it. But it was all superfluous to the fact that she was watching the weather; her ambition was to fly to Inishmore, the largest of the three Aran Islands and, like myself no lover of flying, she was waiting for the 'best day'. It wasn't making itself obvious. Each morning she scanned the sky anxiously for that 'bit of blue' that would give us our chance.

On our second last day she decided it was now or never. An early start and we were at Galway Airport, the new building almost but not quite completed, and so we were brought through a port-a-cabin to be issued with our tickets. We were told that we were very lucky: the Courts were sitting on Inishmore that day and our flight was almost fully booked – by lawyers. And sure enough, in the plane there they were, six besuited gentlemen, briefcases clutched on their knees, and they, the two of us, the pilot and one cabin crew member filled every seat – each seat having been allotted to us after we had been weighed in the port-a-cabin, to get the balance right.

As we trundled down the runway I looked in terror at the tiny wing of the plane just below the window where I was sitting and, in order to try to reassure myself, said to the solemn looking gentleman beside me, 'Are you ever afraid, in this little plane?' He looked down his aquiline nose at me, the epitome of Sean Keating's West of Ireland man, despite his attire, and said severely, 'Certainly not! These are the safest planes in the world!' And he thereupon crossed himself expansively. I quickly followed suit with, I am sure, at least equal fervour, but far less panache.

I plucked up the courage to ask him about the Sitting. It was a knocking-down case, I was informed; a pedestrian had been hit by a bicycle. I asked if the Judge was on the plane. 'Oh no,' my informant told me, 'He never flies; hates it. He's in that boat down there.' He pointed, and I looked out of the window and saw the little boat plying its way through the waters. Did the Judge know more than the rest of us, I wondered?

When we taxied to a halt on the grass runway on Inishmore some ten or twelve minutes after we had left Galway airport, all the lawyers were bundled into a waiting Garda van, and it sped off. That left the two of us to find our own way to Dán Aongus, or so we thought.

But not so. Within minutes Mícheál had arrived in his mini-bus, and he brought us as near as he could to Dún Aongus. From where he left us we continued up the sloping ground, over the same bare limestone terrain which we had experienced in the Burren. And all the while my companion took photos.

Much later in the day, and exhausted, as we were returning to the plane (which we had almost to ourselves, the lawyers having returned to the mainland after an early last-minute settlement) the rain came down in bucketfuls, and we had to take shelter in a ditch. We made a tent out of our plastic macs and watched the water running down the folds in rivulets. I remember that at one point the intrepid pilgrim glanced at me and said, chuckling, 'If only my doctors could see me now!'

Back in the guesthouse that evening the fishy stories at the other six tables continued, one outdoing the other in outrageous exaggeraton. Then a clear, distinctly Germanic voice called over in our direction, 'And what did you two get up to today?' A pause, and then I heard the gleeful voice beside me: 'Oh, we flew to the Aran Islands!'

To our amazement, there was a spontaneous burst of applause! The achievement of having made the trip in poor weather had been enough for us, but the appreciation by others that we had done so did not go amiss. Little could our cheerers have known just what an achievement it had been for one of our party.

Back in Dublin, she phoned me a few days later. 'I have the photos,' she said. 'I'll bring them over.'

One by one she handed them to me, commenting on each.

She looked at the last photo for a long moment before she handed it to me, saying as she did so, 'When I took this, I only saw the flowers, not all the rest.' The photo she handed me was the photo which today graces the cover of this book.

Thus did we come to see the overall picture.